HOW TO INVEST LIKE THE WORLD'S GREATEST INVESTORS

HOW TO INVEST LIKE THE WORLD'S GREATEST INVESTORS

A Fast Guide to Proven Strategies for All Market Conditions

HANS NORÉN

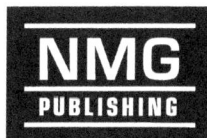

Published by NMG PUBLISHING, Åkerögatan 14, 74563 Enköping, Sweden

Translated from Swedish.

The originals title:
MÄSTARNAS INVESTERINGAR: Hur man bygger en förmögenhet genom att tillämpa samma strategier som de framgångsrikaste investerarna i världen

NMG is a trademark of NMG PUBLISHING

Cover design by Michele DeFilippo, 1106 Design, LLC

Manufactured in the United States of America

ISBN 91-973812-1-7

This publication is designed to provide useful advice in regard to the subject matter covered. It is sold with the understanding that the author and publisher are not engaged in rendering legal, financial or other professional services. If the reader requires expert assistance or legal advice, a competent professional should be consulted.

The author and publisher specifically disclaim any responsibility for liability, loss, or risk, personal or otherwise, that is incurred as a consequence, directly or indirectly, of the use and application of any of the contents in this book.

"Buy when everyone else is selling and hold until everyone else is buying."
J. Paul Getty

Contents

Introduction

What does it take to make money in the stock market? The majority of all professional investors don't beat the Dow Jones Index over time. Over half of all analysts' advice is worthless. Is there a way for an ordinary person to beat the Dow, and thereby do better than the professionals? My answer to that question is yes.

It doesn't take a mathematical genius to make it in the stock market. What it takes is a proven investment strategy and enough discipline to follow that strategy. Most of you readers will probably experience that discipline is your biggest obstacle.

It can be very hard to think independently when you all the time is confronted with opinions that contradict your own opinion. You must stand up for your own view and never give in to public opinions if you want to become a successful investor. Remember, you are never wrong just because everyone else thinks that you are wrong. Knowledge about the markets psychology improves your chances of success.

If you want to be a successful investor you must:

Have an investment strategy that really works

Have discipline

This book is about value investing. A number of well-known investors relays on value investing to succeed. The greatest of them is probably Warren Buffett, one of the richest persons in the World.

WHAT YOU CAN LEARN FROM THIS BOOK

It has been my goal to make this book very much focused and to the point. I have tried to exclude all useless filler text that just takes up your time.

In chapter 1 we will look at the most common investment strategies. We will also see why these strategies don't work very well in real life.

Chapter 2 will give you the basic knowledge of value investing. You will get some of the tools necessary for analysing a company.

The whole chapter 3 is about Warren Buffett. We will see how this legend determines the value of a company. For those who are already familiar with Buffett this chapter can serve as a good repetition.

The psychological aspects of investing will be discussed in chapter 4. We will also look briefly at the historical side of speculation.

There are investment situations when special circumstances must be taken into account. This is the case when you invest in some foreign companies, technology companies and small companies. Chapters 5-7 will deal with those situations.

Chapter 8 is about mutual funds. It is not uncomplicated to choose a mutual fund. Now you will learn how to invest in them the right way.

Chapter 9 is named "Your Personal Investment Style". This book will give you the tools for success. But remember that you will not succeed just by trying to exactly copy someone else's success. In order to succeed you must combine the strategy with your own judgement.

If you want to continue your studies of investing you will find recommendations for further reading in chapter 10. Only the best literature on the subject is good enough.

In Appendix there is information about the stock holdings of mutual funds and companies managed by investors that are being mentioned in this book.

1

Different Investment Strategies: Why Do So Many Intelligent People Only Receive Mediocre Results?

"Those who cannot remember the past are condemned to repeat it"

George Santayana

FUNDAMENTAL AND TECHNICAL ANALYSIS

In stock market analysis there are two major schools, fundamental analysis and technical analysis. Everyone that invests or speculates in the stock market (we will discuss the difference between investing and speculating later in this chapter) is directly or indirectly affected by at least one of these schools.

Fundamental analysis is the traditional way of analysing a stock. Here you look at relevant financial measures.

In technical analysis you try to predict the stocks movement by looking at historical data. The thought is that history will repeat it self. The investment strategy that we will look at in this book is part of the fundamental school.

PROBLEMS WITH TECHNICAL ANALYSIS

Technical analysis does not work in reality! But Technical methods are very popular and there are several books and software programs out there. Many of them promise fantastic results and talks about big profits.

"Our analytical program is the best in the market. The portfolio is up 500% so far this year."

Of course you get interested. But behind the advertising you will often find constructions made up after the market is closed. It is easy to place a bet when the race is over and you know the result.

By looking at a chart you can see how a stock has moved in the past. But to use this information to predict the future is a waste of time. Many things will happen to a company during its lifetime and the fundamental analysis becomes a necessity to determine the company's present status. If you rely on technical analysis you might as well use astrology (and yes, there are people wasting their time on market forecasting with astrology as well).

EMT

Efficient Market Theory, from now on referred to as EMT, is the name on the investment theory that has had the biggest influence on the financial world during the last decades. We are talking about a gigantic influence here. This is what business schools around the world are teaching their students. With an acceptance like that from both the financial and the academic world you might think that this is the way to invest, right? Wrong! *This is not the way to invest!* EMT doesn't work and it is important to know why because so many peoples behaviour in the marketplace is dictated by this theory.

According to EMT the market is always giving a stock a correct valuation, even in the short-term. With that many experts analysing and acting on all the available information the stock must have a correct price in every moment. The only way to beat the market then should be by trading on insider information. And that is illegal.

But the skilled investors who beat the market year after year, how do you explain them? Are they cheating or are they just being lucky? You must also ask yourself how big crashes like the one in 1987 can occur if the market is efficient at all times. Are profitable and well-managed companies, whose stocks are being pushed down by the depressive state of the market, really a much worse investment today compared to yesterday?

RISK

But believers in EMT think that they know a way to actually beat the market. It is done by consider the "risk" involved. They think that risk is the same as volatility. Volatility measures how much the price of a stock moves up and down. The bigger the price movement is the bigger the risk is, according to EMT. This is referred to as Beta.

This way to determine risk is nonsense! Price movements are price movements and nothing else. If a company that is already undervalued goes down by another 20%, because of factors that has nothing to do with the company, is it then more or less safe to invest in it? Is it more or less risky to buy 1 dollar for 20 cent than for 40 cent when the company's fundamentals are exactly the same? For an educated investor the answer is obvious. It is also very uncommon that anyone complains about risk in times when the stock market is extremely bullish.

To buy undervalued stocks with a certain margin of safety is the best way to reduce risk. You will learn how to do this.

MPT

MPT (Modern Portfolio Theory) is based on EMT. Fund managers around the world are using this theory as a base for their investments. The economists who thought that risk was volatility constructed model portfolios with different "risk levels". But what are actually being measured are only the price movements.

The economists like to use complicated mathematical formulas to prove their point. Maybe these formulas have a value of their own in the academic world. But in the real world, where real money is at stake, they can only do damage.

TO PREDICT THE FUTURE

Today the fundamental analysis is focused on growth. By predicting a company's future growth many analysts thinks they can find fantastic opportunities. But how much of a chance is there for *anyone* to predict future earnings? Unfortunately there is only a very small chance.

A lot of companies must be enormously profitable for many years to come in order to motivate its high valuation. Market studies shows that the analysts have a very bad record when it comes to predicting future earnings growth.[1] Maybe we could have hoped that they were wrong so often because their prognoses were conservative. But unfortunately it is the over-optimism that dominates the field completely.

The analysts' error percentage increases in relation to time. It obviously gets worse and worse. A reasonable demand for a prognosis should be that it lands within a 5% margin, up or down. An extensive study shows the odds for predicting 20 quarters within the 5% margin. *The odds are 1 in 50 billions.*[2] You have a better chance to win the lottery. But every day people accept these lousy market odds just because they don't know about them.

Why does anyone continue with something that gives such bad results? Obviously there is a fear of going against the crowd. Only a few people have the guts to think and act independently. If "buy IBM now" is the common opinion in the financial world it can have its price to say something completely different.

A tendency to overrate the personal ability also plays a part as a bad prognosis factor. But I don't think that this is something typical for financial analysts. It is probably the same in other professions but misjudgements there doesn't always have the same direct visibility when it comes to economic consequences.

TO BUY HIGH AND SELL LOW

But why not just buy a popular stock that has gone up much in resent time. The stock has gone through the roof and it will probably continue upwards for a while, or? And you can always avoid a crash by selling in time can't you? Thousands and thousands of small investors thinks exactly like this.

"The strategy" is to buy high and sell even higher. But in reality it almost always ends up with buying high and selling low. In the long run it becomes impossible to just ride on the wave. Last in are often last out and in last place we find the small investors.

INVESTMENT vs. SPECULATION

I believe that the investor always will have an advantage over the speculator. In the long term the investor always wins.

What are the differences between investing and speculating? The legend Benjamin Graham tried to straighten things out in his book *The Intelligent Investor*. According to Graham an investment must mean safety combined with an adequate return. The stock must be thoroughly analysed before an investment can take place. Everything else is speculation.[3] He saw that the term investor was wrongly used for more or less everyone that owned stocks.[4] In the next chapter we will see what a safe investment with adequate return looks like.

You can of course have other safety margins than Graham and still be an investor. But to just buy stocks without any deeper knowledge is nothing more than speculation.

SPECULATION vs. GAMBLING

There are some people that compare speculation in the market with gambling. This comparison is fundamentally wrong and builds on a misconception about the financial markets. We can take a lottery game as an example. The game itself has only one purpose and that is to bring in money to those behind the lottery (often a state). The game exists only for the game.

Speculation on the other hand fills an important function in society by transferring risk to someone who is willing to take it. A farmer might want to protect his revenues from the harvest and, with the help of derivatives, he can insure him self and transfer the risk to a speculator that is willing to take the risk. There will always be speculators because their behaviour is a part of the human nature.

DAY TRADING

In later years we have seen an increasing interest for day trading. An ordinary person with a computer connected to the Internet can now try to compete with professional traders at the brokerage firms. When done correctly day trading is neither investing nor speculating. It is all about being a good trader.

For a person who lacks talent and education I can't think of any opportunity to lose money faster, not even a casino. I recommend anyone who wants to day trade for a living to really educate yourself in the subject matter before you use any real money.

WHAT YOU DON'T LEARN AT BUSINESS SCHOOL

At business schools and universities around the world students learn EMT. They think they can manage risk properly and they master many complicated mathematical formulas that are completely useless when it comes to real life. People who really know how to invest should be happy about this. If real investors graduated from business school the competition in the market place would be much harder.

Hopefully you will avoid using any form of technical analysis from now on, regardless of what kind of return they promise you in the advertising. You also know that risk is not the same thing as volatility. You never buy a stock just because everyone else seems to buy it. And last but not least, you now know how difficult it is to calculate a company's future earnings.

We will now move on and learn how to really find the winning stocks. You will learn...

2

Value Investing

"Price is what you pay. Value is what you get."
Warren Buffett

Value investing is about buying stocks when they are undervalued. In the short-term the market often overreacts. Because of the overreactions there are always stocks that trade at higher or lower prices than they should. But the market is always right in the long run and investors who bought undervalued stocks will see their investments increase in value. It's all about taking advantage of the markets manic-depressive behavior.

HOW TO FIND A STOCK WORTH BUYING

Benjamin Graham probably invented modern financial analysis. Many people claim that there really wasn't anything worth referring to as financial analysis before Graham. Together with David Dodd he wrote the classic *Security Analysis.* The first edition of this book came in 1934. Graham is also the man behind another classic investment book, *The Intelligent Investor.*

Typical for Graham is his focus on finding undervalued assets. He spoke about a "margin on safety". In order to be a safe investment a stock must be bought at a price that is at least 30 % under the company's book value. That 30 % is a safety margin for the investor.

23

We will now look at different methods that can be used to find out if a stock is worth buying. For those of you who have never read an annual report and/or feel insecure about the financial terminology I recommend the book *How to Read a Financial Report* by John A. Tracy.

Methods for finding a stock worth buying:

Low P/E Ratios

Low Price to Cash flow

The Net Net Method

Low Price to Dividend

Low P/E Ratios

The P/E ratio (short for Price/Earnings) is the stocks current price divided with the earnings per share for the latest 12 months.

You will find the P/E ratio in the newspapers. A high P/E ratio indicates that the markets expectations of the company is high, a low P/E ratio indicates the opposite. Some people argue that a high P/E ratio should be seen as a quality label for companies. They must be good when the market believes in them. But an assumption like that also requires you to believe that the market is always right, and in the short term the market is often wrong.

Sometimes you see companies with a P/E ratio higher than 80. These companies are often in high-tech industries that are very difficult to analyse in the first place. They often find it difficult themselves to fully explain what it is they are doing. Companies like this are often "hot" and it seems like everyone wants to invest in them because they are afraid to miss the money train and be left behind at the station. In many cases the company might not even have a P/E ratio because it is unprofitable. That is especially true when it comes to newly introduced companies that referred to themselves as "a new Microsoft" when the IPO was launched.

The question you should ask yourself as an investor is, how long time it will take for the company to earn the kind of money necessary to justify its current P/E ratio? With a high P/E ratio we end up in a distant future. In the previous chapter we saw how difficult it is to predict a company's future earnings. The fact that many of the companies with the highest P/E ratios are in high-tech industries that is very difficult to analyse doesn't make things better. It is no doubt that the P/E ratio is an excellent instrument to use when you want to identify overvalued companies.

But what is a reasonable P/E ratio? At what level is it time to buy? There is no ideal number that can be used on all industries. You will have to look at the P/E ratio for each industry. Pharmaceutical companies, for example, are often traded at significantly higher multiples than manufacturing companies. Graham believed that a company with a P/E ratio of around 20 or higher wasn't a safe investment. But in my eyes it seems a bit drastic to completely exclude the possibility to invest in companies with a P/E ratio of 20 or more.

Many skilled investors have specialized in companies with low P/E ratios. The method is well tested with good results. David Dreman (Appendix 3) is author of the excellent book *Contrarian Investment Strategies.* In this book you can see investigations that clearly show us that companies with low P/E ratios are better investments over time.[1]

Another way to approach the low P/E method is to buy stocks in companies with the lowest P/E ratios in a specific industry. The selection will then be made among the 20 % of companies with the lowest ratios in that industry. This is regardless of how high or low multiples the industry as a whole is traded to. The method has been practiced with good results.[2] This industry approach can also be used on price to cash flow, price to book value, and price to dividend.

Low Price to Cash flow

Buy stocks with a low price to cash flow. *Cash flow is the company's net income (after taxes) plus the amounts written off for depreciation and other noncash charges. Price/Cash flow is the stocks current price divided with the latest fiscal year's cash flow.*

Investors all over the world focus on cash flow. A positive cash flow is an absolute necessity because it makes it possible for the company to pay its overall expenses. It is really true that Cash is King. We will look more at cash flow in the chapter about Buffett.

The Net Net Method

Somewhere you will always find companies that trades below its book value. Of course it is much easier to find them in a bear-market, but opportunities appear even in bull-markets. What we get is a liquidation value for the company.

It is this method that Graham is most famous for. To succeed the investor will have to do some work. You will need an annual report from the company you consider investing in. Annual reports are often available for download on the Internet. Take the company's current assets *and subtract current liabilities and long-term debt. Then divide with the number of outstanding shares and you get the net net asset value per share.*

To fully qualify as safe, according to Graham's margin of safety standard, the stock cannot be bought at price higher than two thirds of the book value. In addition to that Graham also demands that the company must be profitable. Without profitability the investment would be too risky.[3]

On the NYSE the normal valuation of a company is around 3 to 5 times the book value. It takes some ambitious searching in order to find a company that fully measures up to Graham's standard. But it is not wrong to look at book value and having a smaller margin of safety than Graham. The net net method is an investment tool that should not be forgotten.

One thing is certain, if you approach the market with this method during a worldwide depression you can get very wealthy.

The Right Value of a Company

As you have seen it is relatively easy to calculate the liquidation value of a company. But the net net method doesn't answer all questions about a company's value.

Imagine that you were going to sell your own company. Wouldn't you want to get some kind of compensation for all the profits your company are expected to generate during its remaining life? Of course you would. The company's right value is made up of its whole intrinsic value. It can be hard to tell exactly what the intrinsic value should be. In the next chapter we will take a closer look at intrinsic value.

It is certain that we in the future will see more and more companies with very few tangible assets like machines and things like that. Instead the competence of the employees and intangible assets like for example copyrights and trademarks will become more important.

Low Price to Dividend

Buy stocks with a low price to dividend. *Price to dividend is the stocks current price divided with the current annual dividend of the company.*

Dividends used to be an important factor when analysing stocks. Companies that pay a high dividend have traditionally been recommended for widows and orphans. It pays to look at dividend even in today's market.

For people with a constant need of income this is probably a more attractive investment than bonds. Stocks with low price to dividend will give you the best protection in a market downturn.

TO USE THE TOOLS EFFECTIVELY

You now have some tools that will help you find interesting stocks. Some investors choose to focus on only one method. Others use all methods in their analyses and buy the stocks that look best seen over the whole line. You can focus on the whole market or a certain industry. Value Investing gives a great room for individualism.

The final selection of stocks should be done among the 20% with the lowest price in their category.

You must understand that use of the net net method will limit the number of stocks available for investment during a bull market.

MORE HELP TO FIND THE WINNERS

Here are some more help to make the final selection easier and safer:

Check the finances

Try to avoid total collapses

Check the Finances

The importance of a positive cash flow, enough to cover basic expenses is something we have already mentioned. Another thing of interest is the company's debt situation. Fund manager Peter Lynch obviously have a point when he says that a company with no debts can't go bankrupt.[4] Companies with strong finances can continue to pay out high dividends to its shareholders even in tough times.

To learn about a company's debts you look at Debt to Equity. *You get this number by taking all the company's debts and divide them with shareholders equity.* An approximate Debt to Equity of 50% is reasonable for a company.[5]

Try To Avoid Total Collapses

Our objective here is not to try to predict the future or make some kind of a forecast about future profits. But if a company gets into deep trouble, and you can expect the recovery time to be very long, then you should think twice before you buy.

If it still seems like a wise decision to buy even after you made a thorough analysis, then go ahead and be contrarian. Remember that if you get too nervous about a downturn in the market you should be doing something else than investing in stocks.

TIME TO TAKE HOME THE PROFIT

We have now reached one of the key questions, a question all investors are familiar with. When is it time to take home the profit? How much more can the stock go up before you sell it? You can become the best in the world when it comes to identifying and buying undervalued stocks and it will still mean nothing if you don't know how to sell the stocks "right". Never fall in love with a stock, fall in love with a good price.

Time to sell:

When the company no longer is undervalued

After a merger

When a better opportunity comes along

The Company Is No Longer Undervalued

The obvious reason to sell is that the stock no longer is undervalued according to the valuation methods that were used when you bought the stock. The market has "discovered" the stock and sent it right up in the sky. The same analysts that trashed the stock yesterday are now competing about how much they can praise it. You sell the stock now when it has become overvalued.

Mergers

When two companies merge the bigger company that comes out of the merger is supposed to be stronger and more profitable for its shareholders. Bigger is supposed to be better and especially in a bull market many companies choose to grow through mergers.

But will the shareholders automatically benefit from a merger? No they don't. *A merger does not automatically mean that the stockholders will make more money.* To bring two companies together is not an easy task. There will be complications when corporate cultures collide and the awaited synergy effects don't seem to happen. It is often a good idea to *sell* your stocks soon after a merger when the enthusiasm is high and the problems still invisible to the public eye.

Of course there can be times when you should keep your stocks even after a merger. You must look at the situation carefully and then make a decision based on your own judgement.

A Better Opportunity Comes Along

It sometimes happens that a better investment opportunity comes along that makes it worth selling stocks to free up some cash for this better opportunity.

TO TAKE A LOSS

Some deals don't work out the way they are supposed to. This fact is not something an investor can afford to be upset over. Sometimes you win and sometimes you lose, that's the name of the game. Learn from it and move on quickly. The secret here is, not surprisingly, to win more deals than you lose. The central question then becomes, when is it time to take the loss? It is about the difference between patience and wishful thinking.

It is time to take a loss when:

The conditions get much worse

You have made an analytical mistake

The Conditions Get Much Worse

The conditions can sometimes change and get much worse. These new conditions are such that they almost completely put your initial analysis out of date. *When you make a new examination you discover that the company's present status is such that it would be impossible for you to even consider investing in this company today. Under these conditions is it time to take a loss.*

It is important to realise that it's not time to sell just because you think that the market hasn't discovered the stock fast enough. Patience is very important for those who want to experience success. The legendary John Neff exemplifies an investor who can wait a very long time for a stock to go up.

Your Own Analytical Mistake

Sometimes you can put yourself in a difficult situation by accident when you make an analytical mistake. The fact that things don't always turn out the way you expects is one thing. What I am talking a about here is instead the human factor in the form of calculation errors. When things like this happens you have to admit to yourself that you made a mistake and then sell the stock immediately, even if you will lose money and it feels real bad.

To do nothing and just hope that the deal will work out good anyway is not an option here. The stock is bought because of an error and must be immediately removed from the portfolio where it never belonged in the first place.

3

Buffett

It has been helpful to me to have tens of thousands (of students) turned out of business schools taught that it didn't do any good to think."[1]

Warren Buffett

Warren Buffett is one of the richest men in the world. What makes Buffett interesting is that he has built a great deal of his fortune through investments in the stock market. This is something unusual among the worlds richest. Benjamin Graham was Buffett's teacher at The University of Columbia and his influence on Buffett is significant. But Buffett doesn't just copy Graham's methods. Instead he has developed his own style to find value.

Many books have been written about Buffett. For the readers who already are familiar with Buffett's investment style I hope that this chapter at least will be valuable as a good repetition.

BUFFETT'S CAREER

1956 was the year when Buffett started a so-called investment partnership. This is not legally a mutual fund but it works in a similar way. He was running Buffett Partnership until 1969. Between 1957 and 1969 he beat the Dow Jones index with an average of 22 % per year.[2]

Buffett invested his capital in Berkshire Hathaway. This was originally a textile company but today insurance's plays an important part in the company. The insurance business provides Buffett with capital to invest.

Among the non public companies that Berkshire owns we find a big furniture store, a jeweller, the newspaper Buffalo News and See's Candy Shops. The textile businesses closed in 1985.[3]

Berkshires portfolio of publicly traded companies contains several multinational companies like Coca-Cola, Gillette and American Express (See Appendix 1).[4]

Buffett runs his company from Omaha in Nebraska. He sees it as an advantage to keep a certain distance to Wall Street; an environment that he thinks can have a bad influence on an investor. "With enough inside information and a million dollars, you can go broke in a year", says Buffett.[5]

FISHER

Philip Fisher is another person that has had a strong influence on Buffett's thinking. Fisher wrote the classic *Common Stocks and Uncommon Profits.*

The foundation of Fisher's philosophy is to buy stocks that are "outstanding" and then keep them for many years.[6] It is almost never appropriate to sell as long as the companies continue to increase its intrinsic value.[7] According to Fisher it is better to make a few extremely successful investments instead of many good investments.[8] He is definitely not a supporter of short-term investing and diversification.

Buffett had the courage to bet on a few great investments and he acts with a long-term perspective. The results that Buffett achieved show us that Fisher's theories have substance and are valuable.

AN INTERESTING COMPANY TO INVEST IN

In the beginning of his career Buffett applied Graham's methods very strict when he invested. But during the years Buffett has developed his own style and this have resulted in many genial investments. Graham's philosophy is still the base.

An understanding of *how* the company makes its money is very important to Buffett. He never invests in a company he doesn't understand. This has kept him away from technology stocks. Buffett never invests in stocks. Instead he invests in companies and he sees himself as a company owner, not just a stockowner.

TWO CATEGORIES OF COMPANIES

Buffett sees two categories of companies, Commodity and Franchise companies.[9]

A commodity company produces a standardised product or service. This is something that is very easy for other companies to copy and the competition is hard. Examples of industries within the commodity category are the airline industry and the oil industry. Price becomes the most important way to compete here and the consequences of a longer price war can be devastating. It becomes hard to be any smarter than your stupidest competitor when you run a commodity business.

Look at the situation for Airline companies in The United States during the early 1990s. It was a period of time when almost every major national airline company was protected under Chapter Eleven. Buffett himself has been a stockholder in Usair and lost a lot of money. He thinks that the best way to create a small fortune is to begin with a big fortune and then invest in an airline company.

37

When we discuss Franchise companies here we don't refer to a specific business model like, for example, McDonald's. Here the word franchise is a pseudonym for strength and superiority. In professional sport they sometimes talk about franchise players. These are the best players, the ones you build your team around. Franchise companies are the best companies, companies you build your portfolio around.

Franchise companies are often strong because they have achieved something of a consumer monopoly on the market. Coca-Cola Company and Disney are typical examples. Another excellent example is Microsoft (not a Buffett company).

Buffett's ideal investment is like a toll bridge. There is only one bridge and everyone must pass it. The owner is thereby guaranteed a steady income stream that in the long-term will make him rich.

INFLATION

Buffett wants to protect himself against inflation. Some companies can stand inflation better than others and are therefore preferable investments.

Let's make this clearer by looking at an example: Company A makes a yearly profit of $ 20 million. In order to make this profit the company depends on equipment for $ 100 million. Company B also makes a yearly profit of $ 20 million but they depend on equipment for $ 200 million. Now let's assume that prices doubles. Even the two companies profit doubles to $ 40 million. But in order to keep profits at the same level company B are forced to use much more money than company A. Equipment wears out and company B got higher expenses to keep their production intact. Company B will have to come up with $ 400 million while company A gets away with $ 200 million.

We have experienced a time of low inflation recently and many investors might think that they don't have to worry about inflation anymore. But we cannot make the assumption that inflation is a problem of the past. Unfortunately it is in the nature of the political system that inflation will return. That is why it is important to know why some companies handle inflation better than others.

FORGET ABOUT THE ECONOMY AND FOCUS INSTEAD ON THE COMPANIES

Buffett's focus is on the companies. Investors should base their decisions on company analysis instead of economic forecasts. Trying to predict if interest rates will go up or down is much more difficult than using the methods outlined in this book to analysing companies. Academic economic theory often leads you in the wrong direction when it comes to investing.

BUFFETT'S METHODS

Here are some of the methods that Buffett uses when he analyses a company:

Buffett looks at:

Intrinsic value

Owner earnings

Return on shareholders' equity

Use of profits

Look-through earnings

Intrinsic Value

When you talk about intrinsic value you don't mean book value. You want your analyse to give you information about the company's current and future value.

Graham had a formula for intrinsic value, E $(2r+8.5) \times 4.4/Y$. Here, E stands for profit per share, r is the expected earnings growth rate and Y stands for the current yield on AAA corporate bonds. 8.5 are, according to Graham, an appropriate P/E ratio for a company without growth.[10] Buffett never uses this formula. It is difficult to work with formulas like this in real life investment situations.

How do you get to know the intrinsic value of a company without using the formula above or similar formulas? Buffett thinks that it is impossible to exactly calculate the intrinsic value. He defines the intrinsic value as "the discounted value of cash that can be taken out from a company during its remaining lifetime".[11] In the annual report of Berkshire Hathaway from 1994, Buffett gives us an example where he describes the acquisition of the conglomerate Scott Fetcher Inc. This company had a book value of $ 172.6 million when Berkshire Hathaway bought it in 1986. Berkshire paid $ 315.2 million for the company. This was a premium of $ 142.6 million. Between the years of 1986 and 1994 Scott Fetcher made a total profit of $ 55.4 million. During the same period of time the company paid not less than $ 634 million in dividends to Berkshire. As you can see the dividends heavily exceed the profits for this time period. This is possible because the company got an excessive amount of cash. The intrinsic value in Scott Fetcher was the discounted value of the cash that could be taken out from the company.

How to Calculate Owner Earnings

There is no doubt that Mario Gabelli (Appendix 2) is one of the world's greatest investors. Gabelli looks at cash flow when he is analysing a company. *But when calculating cash flow Gabelli realises that it is important to withdraw the capital expenditures that are necessary for the company to grow.*[12]

Now we got something to think about. In the previous chapter we could see the usual definition of cash flow as the company's net income (after taxes) plus the amounts written off for depreciation and other noncash charges.

Instead of cash flow Buffett prefers to talk about owner earnings. The problem with the usual definition of cash flow is, according to Buffett, that it doesn't tells us how much of the net profit that must be used in order to maintain the company's market position.

We can see significant variations between different industries here. Real estate companies have big investment costs in the beginning, but then the costs go down.

Manufacturing companies, on the other hand, might need cash on a regular basis to keep things running. It is clear that the traditional way of looking at cash flow not always will work.[13]

From the company's cash flow Buffett subtracts the expenses and working capital that the company will need to use.[14] To be able to do this properly you will need to have some knowledge about the company. It is not enough to know how the company makes its money. You also need to know the costs for making that money.

Return on Shareholders' Equity

The shareholders' equity in a company is made up of the total assets minus the total liabilities. Buffett looks at the return on shareholders' equity; this is one of his most important methods.

How the return is calculated can be illustrated in the following way: A company got $ 20 million in assets and $ 10 million in liabilities. The shareholders' equity is thereby $ 10 million. The company's profit for the year is $ 2 million. Return on shareholders' equity will be 20% (2,000,000/10,000,000=20%).

The average return on shareholders' equity from an American company during the latest 40 years has been 12%. Buffett is only interested in companies with a rate of return of 15% or more.[15]

How Are The Profits Being Used?

Buffett have said that you only should invest in a company that even an idiot can run because before you know it there is an idiot in charge. A franchise company can survive with an idiot at the top but a commodity company is in serious trouble without competent management.

There is an excellent way to measure the quality of management. Buffett looks at how the disposable profit is being used. Management can choose between reinvesting the profit or give it to the shareholders as dividend. When management choose reinvesting they put their credibility on the *line. Here the thought is that reinvesting shall take place only when this alternative is likely to give the shareholders more money back than they would have got if they invested the money themselves.* If the shareholders can get a 10% return on the money and the management only 5%, then the money should go to the shareholders.

A word of warning is in its place here. It's not always easy to calculate the disposable profit. A successful company that even an idiot can manage is also a very good hiding place for idiots. The big profits make it much easier for management to cover up its mistakes.

Look-Through Earnings

Instead of judging a company only after the price fluctuations of the stock you can calculate look-through earnings.[16] *You do this by multiplying the profit per share with the number of stocks you own in the company*. You now get a good picture of what the stock is worth as a long-term investment. A better picture than the short side of the stock market can give you.

CORPORATE MANAGEMENT

The quality analysis focuses very much on corporate management. Buffett wants the corporate management to act in a rational way. They must be able to cut costs when that is required. Considering his great fortune Buffett himself lives without extreme luxury. The name of Berkshire Hathaway's corporate jet is *The Indefensible* because it can be seen as an indefensible expense.

Good management:

Rational

Sincere

Can act independently

It is also important to Buffett that corporate management is sincere and can act independently. Of course it can be very hard for smaller stockholders to examine if the company leaders have these qualities. A small stockholder can't get close enough to the top. But the small stockholder can observe how willing the CEO is to go public even with his bad deals. If he can admit his mistakes openly that can be a good sign.

If a company is undervalued it makes sense that the company buys back its own stocks. When management decides to buy back stocks they send out signals that they think the company is a good investment and that they want what's best for the stockholders.

HOW TO MANAGE THE PORTFOLIO

When others just see a portfolio of stocks Buffett sees a portfolio of companies. The use of expressions like "owner earnings" shows that he think about himself as the company's owner.

Portfolio management the Buffett way:

Low diversification

Long-term horizon

How many stocks should be part of the portfolio? How much diversification is really necessary? Buffett is not an advocate of diversification. He is willing to bet very much on one card when the right opportunity comes along. If there are 20 investment opportunities available, and you can rank them after attractiveness from 1 to 20, why should you then bet on alternative 20 when there are 19 better opportunities? It will also be harder to monitor the companies close enough if you have too many in your portfolio.

Buffett got a very long-term investment horizon. He has even declared some of his holdings, for example Coca-Cola, as lifetime holdings. These are companies that never will be sold.

A company like Coca-Cola has really proven itself to be the kind of "outstanding" company that Fisher talked about. All this doesn't mean that Buffett completely stays away from short-term transactions. He can also identify special situations in the marketplace that gives the investor an opportunity to reap a quick profit.

TIME TO BUY

The only times when Buffett cares about the stock market itself is when it is time to buy or sell. You can't buy at any price. Even a good company can be too expensive at the moment. First Buffett analyses the company and find out what it is worth, then he looks at the stock market. What's the company's price? It will be time to buy when the valuation is low and you can get a good margin of safety as protection.

Buffett judges the safety margin by himself but the foundation is Graham. The day-to-day life of a successful investor is largely made up of waiting. This waiting can be hard to handle for someone who is used to do a lot of buying and selling. Sometimes the waiting is long. But eventually the depressive side of the market will put an acceptable price tag on your favourite company. The market rewards patience.

TIME TO SELL

You will probably not find many investors that have declared some of their stocks as lifetime holdings. But it must be pointed out that there are only some stocks in Berkshire Hathaway's portfolio that have this status. Even Buffett sells and takes home the profit.

4

Market Psychology

An oil prospector, moving to his heavenly reward, was met by St. Peter with bad news. "You are qualified for residence," said St. Peter, "but as you can see, the compound reserved for oil men is packed. There is no way to squeeze you in." After thinking for a moment, the oil prospector asked if he might say just four words to the present occupants. That seemed harmless to St. Peter, so the oil prospector cupped his hand and yelled, "Oil discovered in hell". Immediately the gates to the compound opened and all the oil men marched out to head for the nether regions. Impressed, St. Peter invited the oil prospector to move in and make himself comfortable. The oil prospector paused. "No", he said. "I think I'll go along with the rest of the boys: There might be some truth to that rumour after all."

A story about the market told by Benjamin Graham.

HUMANS WILL ALWAYS BE THE SAME

The stock market is manic-depressive. *To get the best price you have to be greedy when others are fearful and fearful when others are greedy.* When you study financial history you can't help to notice that humans in some aspects always are the same. We don't know the exact reasons behind this. But one thing is obvious; even though we have much to learn from history most people seems to learn absolutely nothing from it.

CRASHES IN A HISTORICAL PERSPECTIVE

Big crashes often occur after euphoric bull-markets. The attitude during this phase is that you must watch out so you don't miss the train. Not long ago many people took the Internet roller-coaster ride. The crowd was on a desperate hunt for Internet stocks. Then they got burned and sold. In a later phase there might be some great bargains among the Internet companies that survived.

Here are some well-known crashes:

Semper Augustus (The Tulip Bubble), Holland 1637

Rare tulips were bought as investments at prices higher than what most luxury cars costs today. When the crash finally came it was massive. It obviously sounds like a bad joke to invest in tulips. But these investors at least had their tulips to look at which is more than speculators in Internet stocks ended up with.

South Sea Company, England 1720

About a decade later it was time again. South Sea Company had a monopoly on England's trade with the Spanish colonies in West-India and South-America. The company's highest valuation was 500 million pounds sterling; which was roughly 5 times the total amount of cash in the whole Europe. The company's stock eventually fell from 1050 pounds sterling to 129 pounds sterling, down by 88% from its all-time high.[1]

Mississippi Company, France 1720

In France the speculators favourite was Mississippi Company. This company had the France monopoly on trade with North America. The stock had an all time high of 18,000 livres. It later went to 200 livres, down 99%.[2]

The Go-Go Years

In the 1960s the New York Stock Exchange experienced a bull market period referred to as the "Go-Go Years". It is interesting to see that a lot of the hausse was based around technology companies. The goal was to find the next IBM or the next Xerox. There are some similarities between this era and the more recent Internet bubble.

A company that was typical for its time was National Student Marketing. A number of companies with products for the youth market were brought together. Here were for example books and records. A skilled salesman led the company. Every year he predicted big profits for the conglomerate.

Then came the downturn and reality caught up on National Student Marketing and other companies like them. The company's stock went from an all time high of 140 dollar to 3.5 dollar.[3]

It is worth to notice that this company at least tried to look profitable. During the Internet bubble it was enough to paint a clear blue sky of future profits.

HOW TO GET THE PSYCHOLOGY ON YOUR SIDE

You have now seen some historical examples. I can guarantee one thing; the future will not be any better.

People will continue to follow the crowd and hunt for fast money. History will repeat it self again and again and again. No evolution in the world will ever change this. But what can the ordinary investor do to get the market psychology working for him? Below are some points.

The Stock Market Can Close For 5 Years

Imagine that you would buy a stock that you can't sell for 5 years because the stock market will be closed. Before you made such a purchase I am sure you would take the time to make a deeper analyse of this company. In fact you would be much more careful than you usually are when you invest in a stock. 5 years is a very long time when you know that you can't get out if anything goes wrong. An investor like Warren Buffett would continue to produce excellent results even if the stock market closed for a 5-year period.

What I want to do here is give you a different perspective on the importance of the stock market. *For a long-term investor the stock market only exists as a tool to buy and sell stocks. It is only interesting as a marketplace.* The short-term perspective of the market with big ups and downs then becomes relatively uninteresting.

It is the long-term perspective that keeps you on track and shields you from speculation.

Turn Off the Market Noise

It is important that you focus on the companies instead of worrying about the economy. By making this a priority you avoid the market noise that surrounds you almost everywhere. The market noise is everything that can influence your mind so that you might start to doubt your strategy. When you doubt your strategy you can begin to feel a pressure to make the same investment decisions as everyone else. When this happens you are in trouble. Predictions about the economy are always a potential threat to every investor if he listens to them.

The market noise comes from all of the media. You got to be critical to everything you see, hear and read.

The Art of Independent Thinking

It is much more difficult to act independently than it is to learn investment strategies. In all kinds of business related disciplines it is definitely this ability that separates the winners from the losers. Everyone that makes investment decisions has, at least sometime, been influenced to make the wrong decision.

What can you do to strengthen your independent thinking? First you must make sure that you are as well prepared as you possibly can be before you make a deal. This will strengthen your self-confidence and the self-confidence will make it easier for you to follow your own opinion.

The only other cure against destructive influence from outside is probably the awareness of that you are constantly being exposed to it. You will find the market noise not only in all of the media but also among family and friends. It *will* be very hard not to get caught in the trap when all the so-called experts says that the overvalued stock actually is a "good buy" or when all the headlines screams out that "the crisis is here to stay".

I know that many of you will fail here. It will simply be to tough for you when the stock you just bought, a stock that everyone else says is a disaster, goes down by another 30%. You will read about the "crisis" in the newspaper and then sell in panic. The right decision would have been to buy some more stocks.

You who are strong enough and really have the guts to go against the market will make an enormous amount of money over time. The reason that people who doesn't employ optimal investment strategies sometimes can get good results is probably because their mental toughness allows them to buy when everyone else is selling and sell when everyone else is buying.

When Fear Holds You Back

Many times it is fear that keeps the investor from making a profit. Or is greed maybe a better word? You think about the stock you bought at 20 dollar. It is now worth 40 dollar and maybe, just maybe, it can continue to climb. All the facts tell you that this stock is now over-valued and should be sold immediately. But you remain passive. "What if the stock goes up to 60 dollar?" It is this fear of missing a part of the "profit" that brings so many investors in misery.

In order to succeed you must overcome this fear and sell when you should sell. And yes, sometimes the stock will continue up for a while after you sold it. But you can't let this fact bother you. When you have sold the stock, don't follow it for a while, you have no reason.

The New Economy

Generally speaking an investor should not try to make predictions about the markets direction. But when a bull market is coming to an end there are some signs about it that are impossible to ignore.

One of these signs is the talk about "a new economy". Old valuation methods are thought of as to old and therefore invalid. History shows us that the thoughts of "a new economy" will circulate at the end of a bull market period. The motives vary from one time to another. During the latest bubble it was the information technology that was the "reason" behind a new economy. One thing is clear; we will proceed to move towards a post-industrial society where the information technology plays an important role. But the same fundamental economic principles that were valid yesterday will still be valid tomorrow. It is pure nonsense to say that sound valuation models can't be applied on new companies.

Remember that speculation bubbles have always existed. Growth combined with strong finances and profitability is preferable at all times. If you only remember growth and forget about strong finances and profitability then bankruptcy will wait just around the corner.

5

International Investments

"Our country is wherever we are well off."
John Milton

THE BASIC RULES ARE THE SAME

There are several mutual funds that invest in foreign stocks. In many cases they will receive the same mediocre results as they would at home. In some cases the results are a disaster. The emerging market funds, which were popular during the early 1990s, took a deep dive after the initial euphoria. The same happened with the Russian funds during the later part of the 1990s.

Investing in emerging markets takes a lot of knowledge and discipline. With a bad investment strategy, or no investment strategy at all, the disaster always waits around the corner. It is like letting a person without a driver's license drive a cart series car at the highest speed.

The basic rules are the same for domestic and foreign investments. Nevertheless there are some aspects to consider when you invest in foreign stocks. Many people live with the illusion that the natural laws are different in other countries. A concrete example is the high P/E ratios for the Japanese stocks. But to believe that those Japanese P/E ratios by nature are higher than other countries is nothing more than self-deception. It is the Japanese companies that are higher valuated.

55

INTERNATIONAL MARKETS

The globalisation of the economy makes it easier for even a small investor to make money from stock markets all over the world. The Internet is the main force behind this. A smart investor that knows what he searches for can find bargains in many places. The speculator gets a chance to participate in more adventures, take larger risks than ever, and finally lose even more money.

ASPECTS TO ESPECIALLY CONSIDER WHEN YOU INVEST IN FOREIGN COUNTRIES

When you invest abroad you should use the methods that you use at home. We will now look at special aspects of international investments that you must be aware of. You need to be extra careful if a country is completely un-known to you.

International Investments

Be extra careful and suspicious when you invest in emerging markets.

Be aware of currency fluctuations

Look at markets that have shown below Average results for some time.

The company comes first.

Be Extra Careful and Suspicious When You Invest In Emerging Markets

In many of these countries the accounting principles are unclear and the control uncertain. The political risk can often be significant. Companies involved with natural resources like oil can have a low market value in countries that once belonged to the Soviet Union. At the same time there is a risk that these resources will be socialised by the governments. Don't misunderstand me; I am not saying that you should avoid these countries. But an awareness of the potential obstacles is a must if you want to make balanced investment decisions.

The advantages of investing in emerging markets are many. The growth rates are often extremely high. There is also a fact that over 85 % of the world's population lives in these countries.[1]

Be Aware of Currency Fluctuations

Investing in foreign countries often means exposure to currency fluctuations. This is something that is already clear to people who invested in the Asian tiger markets in the 1990s.

Bigger companies and institutions protect themselves from fluctuating currencies through hedging. This means that they use derivatives to insure the currency to avoid losses. Hedging is an insurance that obviously costs money. For a value investor hedging is not an optimal solution. The reason is that it can be very difficult to predict the length of the investment time. The "insurance cost" will therefore be very difficult to predict.[2]

Look At Markets That Have Shown Below Average Results for Some Time

Look at markets that have shown below average results only to get an indication of where in the world you can buy undervalued stocks. There are many opportunities to find stocks on sale. Value investing is practiced mostly in the United States. When you use the methods in other markets there should be interesting opportunities revealed.

The Company Comes First

Never buy a stock just because the country where the stock is traded is "popular" among other investors. Beware of the crowd. It is the company's valuation that is important. You buy stocks in the company, not the country.

ADRs

ADRs (American Depositary Receipts) are an interesting alternative. An ADR is a certificate that represents the value of a foreign stock. ADRs are traded on the US markets. They are traded in, and pay dividends in US dollars.

A clear advantage with these certificates is that the Security and Exchange Commission (SEC) view them, in some aspects, as American assets. They are subject to a certain control and that makes them a bit safer. ADRs make it easier to invest in, for example, Russian stocks.

6

Technology Companies

"Offence wins matches, defence wins championships."
A statement that is true even outside the world of sports.

GARP

Technology companies can look very different when you compare them to other companies. It is often difficult to fully understand what they do. These companies will often have a high valuation. In some cases the valuations are insane. During a bull market many of the technology-oriented companies have a P/E ratio that directly disqualifies them as investment opportunities.

But when the market overreacts in the other direction, and the prices go down to more reasonable levels, it is possible to find so-called GARP- Growth at Reasonable Price. If you can buy growth at a reasonable price it is often a great buy. This is true for all growth-oriented industries.

The Strongest Survives

You must understand that it is the bad times that separate the winners from the losers. A Company, technology oriented or not, really proves something when it can show a decent growth in earnings even during tough market conditions.

Many companies that are involved in new technologies did not even made a profit during the bull-market times when they where started. Maybe they managed to grow anyway through mergers and acquisitions, but that time is over now. An investor who applies value investing methods doesn't have to worry about those losers because they didn't meet his investment criteria's in the first place.

But isn't it the stock markets role in the first place to provide new and exiting companies with capital? Yes, it is true that this is very important. And one thing is clear, there have always been speculators willing to take risks and there always will be. Leave the gambling to others and concentrate instead on the methods that *will* make you rich.

WANGER

Legendary investor Ralph Wanger is known for skilled investments in smaller companies. A person that invested 10,000 dollars in his investment fund in 1970 could see that his capital had grown to 618,000 dollars in 1996. USA Today asked a group of prominent investors who they would like to see managing their own wealth. Wanger won before Buffett.

Wanger believes that instead of investing in a company that makes a certain product it is better to invest in a company that benefits from that products existence. Instead of investing in a company that makes video game machines you invest in the company that makes the video game software. Wanger has for example owned stocks in Electronic Arts.[1] Bill Gates is the richest man in the world because Microsoft is the biggest on operative systems for computers. He wouldn't be that rich if Microsoft instead had built the computers.

In his book *A Zebra in Lion Country* Wanger gives historical examples to explain his view. The big railroad companies who linked the American continent together eventually faced financial difficulties. Many of them went bankrupt. A city like Chicago experienced a big expansion thanks to the railroads and the investors who bought land in the region made big money.[2] If they instead had bought railroad stocks they would have gone broke.

7

Small Companies

"Dumbo could fly because he was a baby elephant. Adult elephants are aerodynamically unsound."[1]
Ralph Wanger

SMALL COMPANIES: THE KEY TO SUCCESSFUL INVESTMENTS?

Are small companies' better investments than larger companies? They can be if you follow certain rules:

Small Companies

Invest only in financially strong companies.

Look at companies with a growth rate above average.

Avoid companies that have never made a profit.

Diversify

Be patient.

Invest Only In Financially Strong Companies

When you look at small companies it is more important than ever to check the finances. *Divide the company's total debts with the shareholders equity.* I mentioned in chapter 2 that an approximate Debt to Equity of 50% is reasonable for a company. You must demand at least the same from a small company.

Look At Companies with a Growth Rate above Average

Companies with a growth rate above average are always interesting. But remember that you are not willing to overpay for that growth.

Avoid Companies That Have Never made a Profit

This is important! Always avoid companies that have never made a profit. A person who buys stocks in a company that has never been profitable is a speculator, not an investor.

Diversify

A portfolio with small companies should be more diversified than a portfolio with bigger companies. Exact how many companies that should be in the portfolio is a matter of individual judgement.

Be Patient

If you follow the advises in this chapter, then you will have a great chance to get an above average return from your small companies portfolio. But it is very important to be patient and have a long-term perspective when you invest in small companies.

A NASDAQ WARNING

Beware of stocks that are rarely traded. You could otherwise face trouble when you want to sell your stocks. This is a problem that exists and you must know about it.

WANGER AND SMALL COMPANIES

Ralph Wanger is also considered to be an authority when it comes to small companies. His concept for success is to find small companies that have found a niche; it can be in technology, but also in marketing where the company is a little bit better than the competitors to sell its products. The company should not be too small according to Wanger. Strong finances are also important. An entrepreneurial management style is something positive. In a large company you talk to an employed CEO. In a small company you talk to the owner.[2]

Wanger points out that a small company have more space for growth. A small software company can triple its sales and make the stock price go through the roof. General Motors on the other hand, can't sell twice as many cars this year as they did last year.

There is more than one way to get a return from a small company. It can happen through growth, re-valuation or a takeover bid. Even bigger companies get bought up but the odds are lower for smaller well-managed companies.[3]

8

Mutual Funds

**"You wonder why fund managers can't beat the S&P 500?
Because they're sheep, and sheep get slaughtered."**
Gordon Gekko (Michael Douglas) in the movie *Wall Street*

Many people own their stocks indirectly through a mutual fund. Mutual funds can in some cases be an alternative to direct ownership of stocks.

Are mutual funds something to recommend for all people who are not interested in investments? Many people thinks so but I disagree. *It takes knowledge to pick the right mutual fund.* If you make the wrong choice your pension money might very well become toys in the hands of a 25-year old speculative fund manager. Maybe he just graduated from business school and when you ask him for his strategy he says something like, "mobile Internet seems to be a real cool investment at the moment".

How do you choose a great mutual fund then? There are several factors to take into consideration. You got to get the answers to some important questions:

> **To Choose the Right Mutual Fund**
>
> What kind of merits does the current fund manager have?
>
> Which investment strategy does the fund manager use?
>
> Which stocks does the mutual fund own right now?
>
> What happens if the fund manager quits?
>
> What are the fees?

WHAT KIND OF MERITS DOES THE CURRENT FUND MANAGER HAVE?

The point of buying into a mutual fund is to have a fund manager that does a better job with your money than you are capable of yourself because you lack the knowledge, or the time. It is the management you pay for and your expectations should be high. It is not enough to look at what the fund have accomplished in the past. You must for example know if the fund always has had the same management. If the fund has a new manager you must check up his track record.

WHICH INVESTMENT STRATEGY DOES THE FUND MANAGER USE?

Find out which investment strategy the fund manager use. Is this strategy the same as your strategy? If it isn't then the fund is not an option for you.

WHICH STOCKS DOES THE MUTUAL FUND OWN RIGHT NOW?

Study the current holdings of the fund. Are the stocks valued high or low in today's market? You got to get an opinion about whether it is the right time to buy into the fund. To buy into an overvalued fund is no better than to buy an overvalued stock.

WHAT HAPPENS IF THE FUND MANAGER QUITS?

Let's say that you have found a well-managed fund with shares at a reasonable price. A question that comes up now is what's going to happen if the fund manager quits. Will the fund's new management continue to use the same investment strategy?

WHAT ARE THE FEES?

The fees are what you pay to get a professional management of your capital. To have low fees as the number one criteria when you search for a good mutual fund will lead you in the wrong direction. Fund-managers that totally focus on fees might very well be believers in EMT. They think that the only way to compete is by offering low fees. That point of view is logical only if you believe that it is impossible to beat index in the long run and that skill has nothing to do with it. Quality costs money. The fact that a skilled manager can take out a higher fee for his services must be consider as something absolutely normal in a free market economy.

Of course the fees do matter when you choose between two funds of equal quality. A skilled manager should be

71

willing to work on a performance basis. He then makes good money only when the customer makes good money.

INDEX FUNDS

Someone who really hates to think about stocks and investments will probably not read this book. If you know someone like that you can recommend this person to consider index funds as an alternative to the bank account. This form of investment makes it possible for the totally ignorant to participate in a market rally, without making any active investment decisions or being in the hands of incompetent fund managers.

Index funds:

Stupid managers can't practice their own stupid ideas here

Passive management should mean lower fees

An index fund is tied to an index, often a stock market index, like for example the S&P 500. If the market goes up the fund will go up and vice versa. Index funds must be seen as long-term investments because no one knows what will happen with the market in the short term.

When you choose an index fund you should look at the fees and search for the lowest possible fees. An index fund is not a complicated product. A computer can more or less manage it so you should not pay anything for the manager's skill in these cases.

Index funds are only recommended to persons who really aren't interested in investing. They are not an alternative to the time-proven strategies you have learned in this book.

9

Your Personal Investment Style

"The secret of success is constancy of purpose."
Benjamin Disraeli

10 YEARS AGO

Let's look back in time for a moment. 10 years ago, what was the economic climate like back then and how did your own economic situation look like at that time? During the first years of the 1990s we experienced a rather depressive side of the market. Then things turned and the decade as a whole must be described as manic.

During the initial phase of this millennium we have experienced the burst of the Internet bubble. An experienced investor expected this bubble to burst and didn't lose any money on Internet stocks. Many of you who did lose money on Internet stocks have now got the ability to avoid the next bubble (it will happen again and again but we don't know in what industries). That is because you have decided to start educating yourself. And by reading this book you are well on you're way to becoming an intelligent investor.

We have also seen that the market system is strong enough to resist terrorist attacks. We cannot allow ourselves to let the fear of terrorist attacks prevent us from taking necessary investment decisions. The show must go on, and it will.

Now let's look forward. How big will your fortune be 10 years from now? You decide that. Take a moment and write down your financial goal. Remember that you can no longer blame the "unpredictable market". Luck and bad luck have very little to do with it. Your results *will* be better than average when you consistently use a time-tested investment strategy.

The downturns will not bother you that much anymore. Instead you will be grateful for the buying opportunities that occur in a bear market.

COMPOUND INTEREST

Sooner or later the party always comes to an end. The bad news is that it must be consider an historical exception to have a market that goes up by more than 20% every year. The good news is that you don't need that kind of increase to make a good result.

A few percentages make a bigger difference than one might expect. Someone who invests his savings and gets a 4% yearly return has doubled his money in 18 years. Someone who invests his savings and gets a 12% yearly return has doubled his money in 6 years.

Albert Einstein believed that compound interest was the greatest invention that's ever been made. It doesn't take a genius to appreciate its positive effects.

STOCKS ARE BEST IN THE LONG RUN

Are stocks really the best investment-form in the long run? The answer is yes, if you invest and not speculate. Bonds don't have a chance against stocks in the long run. It is also a myth that bonds are such a safe investment. Bonds give a bad protection against high inflation. This doesn't mean that you as an investor never should buy bonds. There are times, especially if stock market valuations are very high, when bonds are the only reasonable alternative.

Index funds are primarily suitable for people with none or little desire to learn how to invest. I don't consider these products to be genial or even sophisticated. My reason for mentioning them in this book is that I see them as an alternative to incompetent mutual fund managers. Watch out for incompetent stockbrokers and fund managers, there are unfortunately plenty of them. The more they promise the bigger reason for you to be sceptical.

SECRETS OF VALUE INVESTORS

In this book I have shown you investment strategies used by the real masters in the world of investing. If you want to know more about these methods you should read the books recommended to you in chapter 10. Materials to analyse, like annual reports, can be ordered direct from the companies and can also in many cases be downloaded from the Internet.

In the appendixes you find information about portfolio holdings of some of the greatest names in value investing. Here are companies from many different industries. A warning is in its place here; don't buy these stocks just because a famous investor has bought them. You must understand the investment you made so that you, for example, know when it is time to sell. Think independently and develop your own style instead of just imitating others.

TO KNOW SOMETHING THAT NOBODY ELSE KNOWS

To know something that nobody else knows is the key to success. Aristoteles Onassis said that and I must agree. Now, when you have read this book, you got knowledge's that a majority of the people in the marketplace have not. Take advantage of this and use your knowledge!

10

The Best Books On Investing

To become a successful investor you must always be willing to educate yourself further. In this chapter I will introduce you to some of the best books on the subject investing.

Buffett: The Making of an American Capitalist

Author: Roger Lowenstein
Publisher: Main Street Books, Doubleday
ISBN: 0-385-48491-7

This is a complete biography where we get to follow Warren Buffett and see how he evolves to become the most successful investor in the world. The book is of extra interest to those who already have some basic knowledge of Buffett's investment strategies.

The author, Roger Lowenstein, is a reporter at *The Wall Street Journal*.

A Zebra in Lion Country: Ralph Wanger's Investment Survival Guide

Author: Ralph Wanger
Publisher: Simon & Schuster

ISBN: 0-684-82970-3

Ralph Wanger (The Acorn Funds) is one of the most successful portfolio managers in the world. His book with
the somewhat odd title is also world class. Here are the
advices you need to become a winner in the investment
jungle.

Contrarian Investment Strategies: The Next Generation

Author: David Dreman
Publisher: Simon & Schuster
ISBN: 0-684-81350-5

This is a well-documented book. The word contrarian
means going against the crowd. In this case it is about
going against the market. After his books on the subject
David Dreman is definitely one of the persons that are
best known for contrarian thinking.

  Dreman is chairman of Dreman Value Management,
LLC. He is also a columnist at *Forbes Magazine*.

The Intelligent Investor

Author: Benjamin Graham
Publisher: Harper & Row
ISBN: 0-06-015547-7

This is a real classic. The first edition of *The Intelligent
Investor* came as early as 1949. The book is a must read
for every person who is serious about investing. Graham
also wrote *Security analysis* together with David Dodd.

The Money Masters

Author: John Train
Publisher: HarperCollins
ISBN: 0-88730-638-1

John Train writes about some very successful investors and one speculator. The chapter about Stanley Kroll shows you how a speculator thinks and acts.

Train is the founder of Train, Smith Investment Counsel.

The New Money Masters

Author: John Train
Publisher: HarperCollins
ISBN: 0-88730-637-3

This is the sequel to *The Money Masters* where Train, after the same concept, writes about successful investors. Don't let the title mislead you; this book is not about some newcomers. Here are only experienced names. But George Soros is really more of a speculator than an investor.

APPENDIX

Appendix 1: Berkshire Hathaway, common stocks portfolio (December 31, 2003)

Company	Number of Stocks	Value
American Express Company	151,610,700	$ 7,312
The Coca-Cola Company	200,000,000	10,150
The Gillette Company	96,000,000	3,526
H&R Block, Inc.	14,610,900	809
HCA Inc.	15,476,500	665
M&T Bank Corporation	6,708,760	659
Moody's Corporation	24,000,000	1,453
PetroChina Company Limited	2,338,961,000	1,340
The Washington Post Company	1,727,765	1,367
Wells Fargo & Company	56,448,380	3,324
Others		4,682
	Totally:	$ 35,287

Note: dollar amounts are in millions.

Source: Berkshire Hathaway Annual Report 2003.

85

Appendix 1 (a): Berkshire Hathaway, earnings per share

Year	Earnings per share
1999	$ 1,025
2000	2,185
2001	521
2002	2,795
2003	5,309

Source: Berkshire Hathaway Annual Report 2003.

Appendix 2: The Gabelli Asset Fund, selected holdings (December 31, 2003)

Company	Number of stocks	Value
Cablevision Systems Corp.	2,035,000	$ 47,598,650
Dana Corp.	570,000	10,459,500
Deere & Co.	400,000	26,020,000
Energizer Holdings Inc.	345,000	12,958,200
InterActiveCorp	850,000	28,840,500
Liberty Media Corp.	4,650,000	55,288,500
Navistar International Corp.	560,000	26,818,400
Neiman Marcus Group Inc.	660,000	33,000,000
News Corp. Ltd. Pfd.	14,000	505,400
Time Warner Inc.	1,400,000	25,186,000

Source: The Gabelli Asset Fund Annual Report 2003.

Appendix 2 (a): The Gabelli Value Fund Inc., selected holdings (December 31, 2003)

Company	Number of stocks	Value
AutoNation Inc.	770,000	$ 14,144,900
Cablevision Systems Corp.	2,725,000	63,737,750
Dana Corp.	1,110,000	20,368,500
Del Monte Foods Co.	230,000	2,392,000
Energizer holdings Inc.	370,000	13,897,200
Gaylord Entertainment Co.	220,000	6,567,000
Navistar International Corp.	560,000	26,818,400
Scripps (E.W.) Co.	159,000	14,968,260
Telephone & Data Systems Inc.	565,000	35,340,750
Waste Management Inc.	400,000	11,840,000

Source: The Gabelli Value Fund Annual Report 2003.

Appendix 3: Scudder-Dreman High Return Equity Fund, the 10 largest holdings (November 30, 2003)

Company	Number of Stocks	Value
Altria Group, Inc	9,001,175	$ 468,061,100
Freddie Mac	5,272,250	286,915,845
Washington Mutual, Inc.	5,947,664	272,462,488
Fannie Mae	3,329,350	233,054,500
UST, Inc.	5,754,300	207,097,257
Bristol-Myers Squibb Co.	7,267,850	191,507,847
ConocoPhillips	3,193,573	181,203,332
JR Reynolds Tobacco Holdings, Inc.	2,908,331	160,539,871
Electronic Data Systems Corp.	6,827,511	147,610,788
ChevronTexaco Corp.	1,639,567	123,131,481

Source: Scudder-Dreman High Return Equity Fund Annual Report 2003.

Appendix 3 (a): Scudder-Dreman Small Cap Value Fund, the 10 largest holdings (November 30, 2003)

Company	Number of Stocks	Value
American Financial Realty Trust (REIT)	680,300	$ 11,565,100
Newcastle Investment Corp. (REIT)	388,759	9,524,595
Ultra Petroleum Corp.	459,800	8,763,788
Triad Hospitals, Inc.	234,000	8,096,400
Loew's Corp. – Carolina Group	326,400	7,539,840
Reliant Resources, Inc.	1,146,700	7,522,352
Precision Castparts Corp.	179,500	7,273,340
Moog, Inc. "A"	165,500	7,199,250
Selective Insurance Group, Inc.	211,300	6,848,233
Tesoro Petroleum Corp.	528,700	6,703,916

Source: Scudder-Dreman Small Cap Value Fund Annual report 2003.

Notes

Chapter 1: Different Investment Strategies: Why Do So Many Intelligent People Only Receive Mediocre Results?

1. David Dreman, Contrarian Investment Strategies: The Next Generation, (New York: Simon & Schuster, 1998), pp. 90

2. David Dreman, Contrarian Investment Strategies: The Next Generation, (New York: Simon & Schuster, 1998), p. 112

3. Benjamin Graham, The Intelligent Investor, 4th ed. (New York: Harper & Row, 1973), p. 1

4. Benjamin Graham, The Intelligent Investor, 4th ed. (New York: Harper & Row, 1973), p. 2

Chapter 2 Value Investing

1. David Dreman, Contrarian Investment Strategies: The Next Generation, (New York: Simon & Schuster, 1998), pp. 142

2. David Dreman, Contrarian Investment Strategies: The Next Generation, (New York: Simon & Schuster, 1998), pp. 194

3. Charles H. Brandes, Value Investing Today 2nd ed. (New York: McGraw-Hill, 1998), p. 58

4. Janet Lowe, Value Investing Made Easy, (New York: McGraw-Hill, 1996), p. 32

5. Janet Lowe, Value Investing Made Easy, (New York: McGraw-Hill, 1996), p. 32

Chapter 3 Buffett

1. Janet Lowe, Warren Buffett Speaks, (New York: John Wiley & Sons Inc., 1997), p. 94

2. Robert G. Hagstrom, JR., The Warren Buffett Way, Investment Strategies of the World's Greatest Investor, (New York: John Wiley & Sons Inc., 1995), p. 4

3. Robert G. Hagstrom, JR., The Warren Buffett Way, Investment Strategies of the World's Greatest Investor, (New York: John Wiley & Sons Inc., 1995), pp. 5

4. Robert G Hagstrom, JR., The Warren Buffett Way, Investment Strategies of the World's Greatest Investor, (New York: John Wiley & Sons Inc., 1995), pp. 6

5. Janet Lowe, Warren Buffett Speaks, (New York: John Wiley & Sons Inc., 1997), p. 67

6. John Train, The Money Masters, (New York: Harper & Row, 1980), p. 66

7. John Train, The Money Masters, (New York: Harper & Row, 1980), p. 78

8. John Train, The Money Masters, (New York: Harper & Row, 1980), p. 64

9. Robert G Hagstrom, JR., The Warren Buffett Way, Investment Strategies of the World's Greatest Investor, (New York: John Wiley & Sons Inc., 1995), pp. 78

10. Janet Lowe, Value Investing Made Easy, (New York: McGraw-Hill, 1996), p. 56

11. Janet Lowe, Value Investing Made Easy, (New York: McGraw-Hill, 1996), p. 15

12. The Gabelli Value Fund Annual Report, 1999, p. 3

13. Robert G Hagstrom, JR., The Warren Buffett Way, Investment Strategies of the World's Greatest Investor, (New York: John Wiley & Sons Inc., 1995), p. 90

14. Robert G Hagstrom, JR., The Warren Buffett Way, Investment Strategies of the World's Greatest investor, (New York: John Wiley & Sons Inc., 1995), p. 90

15. Mary Buffett – David Clark, Buffettology, (New York: Rawson Associates, 1998), p. 105

16. Robert G Hagstrom, JR., The Warren Buffett Way, Investment Strategies of the World's Greatest Investor, (New York: John Wiley & Sons Inc., 1995), p. 266

Chapter 4 Market Psychology

1. David Dreman, Contrarian Investment Strategies:
   The Next Generation, (New York: Simon & Schuster,
   1998), p. 371

2. David Dreman, Contrarian Investment Strategies:
   The Next Generation, (New York: Simon & Schuster,
   1998), p. 371

3. David Dreman, Contrarian Investment Strategies:
   The Next Generation, (New York: Simon & Schuster,
   1998), p. 371

Chapter 5 International Investments

1. Charles H. Brandes, Value Investing Today, 2nd ed.
   (New York: McGraw-Hill, 1998), p. 108

2. Charles H. Brandes, Value Investing Today, 2nd ed.
   (New York: McGraw-Hill, 1998), p. 139

Chapter 6 Technology Companies

1. Ralph Wanger, A Zebra In Lion Country, (New
   York: Simon & Schuster, 1997), p. 127

2. Ralph Wanger, A Zebra In Lion Country, (New York:
Simon & Schuster, 1997), pp. 127

Chapter 7 Small Companies

1. Ralph Wanger, A Zebra In Lion Country, (New York: Simon & Schuster, 1997), p. 34

2. Ralph Wanger, A Zebra In Lion Country, (New York: Simon & Schuster, 1997), p. 28

3. Ralph Wanger, A Zebra In Lion Country, (New York: Simon & Schuster, 1997), pp. 34

Glossary

ADRs (American Depositary Receipts)

An ADR is a certificate that represents a foreign stock.

Beta

The beta theory is about a stocks price movement. If a stock have a beta value over 1 it will react relatively more than market index. If a stock has a beta value less than 1 it will react relatively less than market index.

Cash flow

Cash flow is the company's net income (after taxes) plus the amounts written off for depreciation and other non-cash charges.

Commodity Company

A company that produces standardised products and/or services that is easy for their competitors to copy.

Consumer Monopoly

Genuine consumer monopolies are like toll bridges. Those who doesn't swim or take the boat will have to pay the fee.

Day trading

A day trader Buy and sell in order to make immediate profits. The operative word here is trading. Day traders are called day traders because they rarely keep their stocks over night.

Derivatives

A derivative is a financial instrument whose return derives from an underlying asset, for example stocks or currencies. The most common derivative is options.

Diversifying

When you diversify you are putting your eggs in more than one basket. You are spreading the risk when you invest in more than one company.

Emerging-market

This is the market in a country characterised as a development country. There are opportunities for high growth, but also risk.

EMT (Efficient Market Theory)

This is an Academic theory that says that the market always values a stock correctly, even in a short-term perspective.

Franchise Company

A franchise company have built-in strength. The company have often reached a consumer monopoly in the market.

Fundamental analysis

Fundamental analysis is the traditional way of valuing a company. Here you look at the balance sheet and relevant financial measures.

Gambling

Gambling is not the same as speculation. Gambling only fills the function of enjoying the gamblers. Speculation got a higher purpose because it transfers risk from someone who needs to protect himself to the speculator.

GARP (Growth At Reasonable Price)

Growth companies traded at a reasonable price.

Hedge

This is a way to insure the investments. You can use derivatives to insure your portfolio.

Index fund

An index fund is tied to an index and follows that index. The management of an index fund is passive.

Inflation

Inflation is the overall general upward price movement of goods and services in an economy.

Insider Trading

When someone, who got information about a security that is not available to the public, trades in this security. The specific legal definition of insider trading varies between different countries.

Intrinsic Value

A company's intrinsic value is a subjective number. Warren Buffett's definition of intrinsic value is the discounted value of the cash that can be taken out from a company during its lifetime.

Investor

An investor is someone who seeks safety combined with good return. The investment object must be carefully analysed before it can be bought.

Margin of Safety

An investor must have a security margin. According to Benjamin Graham the price you pay for a stock should be at least 30 % below the company's book value. The company must also be profitable if you want it to qualify as a safe investment.

MPT (Modern Portfolio Theory)

The Modern Portfolio Theory builds on EMT. This is about portfolio constructions with different levels of "risk". But what's actually being measured here is not risk but volatility.

The Net Net Asset Value

The net net asset value per share is the company's current assets minus current liabilities and long-term debts, divided with the number of outstanding shares.

Option

An option gives the right (or obligation) to buy or sell something in the future at a determined price.

P/E Ratio (Price-to Earnings)

The stocks current price divided with earnings per share for the latest 12 months.

Portfolio

An investment portfolio is the combined holdings of an investor.

Price to Dividend

The stocks current price divided with the current annual dividend.

Prognosis

In a prognosis you try to predict the future.

Quality Oriented Analysis

Here the focus is on other aspects than the numbers. A quality-oriented approach is suitable when analysing the corporate management.

SEC (Security and Exchange Commission)

An American government agency that regulates American security exchanges.

Speculator

The speculator is willing to take chances without doing a complete analyse before he buys. The speculator is the opposite of the investor.

Technical Analysis

Technical analysis is an attempt to predict the stocks future direction by looking at historical data.

Value Investing

A form of fundamental analysis that focuses on finding undervalued companies.

Volatility

Price-movements.

Index

F

Fisher, Philip, 36, 45
Forbes Magazine, 80
Franchise companies, 37-38, 42
Fundamental analysis, 15, 18

G

Gabelli, Mario, 41
Gambling, 20, 62
GARP (Growth at Reasonable Price), 61
Gekko, Gordon, 69
  (see also Douglas, Michael)
General Motors, 67
Getty, John Paul, 5
Gillette, 36
Go-Go years, the, 49
Graham, Benjamin, 20, 23, 25, 27, 35, 37, 40, 46, 47, 80

H

HarperCollins, 81
Harper & Row, 80
Hedging, 58
How to Read a Financial Report, 24
  (see also Tracy, John A.)

I

IBM, 19, 49
Indefensible, 44
Index, 11, 35, 71
Index fund, 72-73, 77

Intelligent Investor, The, 20, 23, 80
  (see also Graham, Benjamin)
Inflation, 38-39, 76
Interest rate, 39
International investments, 55-59
Internet, 21, 27, 48, 49, 56, 69, 75, 77
Intrinsic Value, 27-28, 36, 40-41
IPO, 25

K

Kroll, Stanley, 81

L

Larger companies, 65
Look-through earnings, 40, 43
Lowenstein, Roger, 79
Lynch, Peter, 29

M

Main Street Books, Doubleday, 79
Manic-depressive, 23, 47
Margin of Safety, 18, 27, 46
Manufacturing companies, 25, 42
McDonald's, 38
Mergers, 31, 62
Microsoft, 38, 62
Milton, John, 55

The Author

The author, Hans Norén, is a successful investor himself with long experience in the stock market. He now shares his insights in the field through this book.

www.ingramcontent.com/pod-product-compliance
Lightning Source LLC
Chambersburg PA
CBHW071505200326
41519CB00019B/5877